AGELESS TIME

CLAIRE ELIZABETH GROSE

Copyright © 2022 by Claire Elizabeth Grose

Compiled and edited by Michael Grose and June Kennedy

All rights reserved. No portion of this publication may be reproduced, stored in a retrieval system or transmitted in any form by any means – electronic, mechanical, photocopying, recording, or any other –except for brief quotation in printed reviews, without the prior written permission of the publisher.

Unless indicated otherwise, all scripture quotations in this book are from the following source:

The Good News Bible: The Bible in Today's English Version (TEV) © 1976 by the American Bible Society. Used with permission.

ISBN 978-0-6486884-8-8

Author contact information - clairegrose.heartmatters@gmail.com

Version 1.0

DEDICATION

This book is dedicated to Lynne and family
My beloved brother

CONTENTS

DEDICATION	IV
CONTENTS	V
PREFACE	VIII
ACKNOWLEDGEMENTS	X
PART ONE	1
MY DAILY PRAYER	4
THE WONDERS OF THIS WORLD	5
THE GLORY OF SUNRISE	6
HOUR GLASS	7
KNOWING YOU IS LOVING YOU	8
PEACE IN MY HEART	9
NO BOUNDARIES	10
APPOINTED TIME	11
PERFECT	14
LOVE HIM	15
MY PEACEFUL HEART	16
UNTARNISHED LOVE	17
REFLECTION OF THE HEART	18
SPREADING HIS LOVE	19
HEAVEN'S GIFTS	20
FACE TO FACE	21
THANK YOU FATHER GOD	22
GOD'S TRUE LOVE	23
UNSPEAKABLE LOVE	26
ABUNDANT LOVE	27
PAGES OF MY HEART	28
CLING TO HIS LOVE	29
PART TWO	30
HEALING WILL UNFOLD	33
WHITE BUTTERFLIES	34
BE MY VOICE	35
HIS PATH	36

I NEED YOU LORD	*37*
KEEP A FAITHFUL HEART	*38*
VALUES OF THE HEART	*41*
YOUR LIGHT	*42*
I'M SO GLAD I'M YOURS LORD	*43*
CROSS THE BRIDGE TODAY	*44*
I'M FOLLOWING YOU LORD	*45*
FIND A SAFE PLACE	*46*
LIFE'S PRESSURES	*49*
HUMANITY	*50*
LIVING IN TRUST	*51*
LIVE BY THE HEART	*52*
LESSONS OF LIFE	*53*
LISTEN TO YOUR HEART	*54*
SAY "YES" TO JESUS	*57*
MY CONSTANT COMPANION	*58*
NEVER GIVE UP	*59*
PILLAR OF LIGHT	*60*
RISE ABOVE YOUR FEARS	*61*
LOVE HIM WITH ZEAL	*62*
WORTHY OF YOUR NAME	*63*
RISE IN HIS GLORY	*64*
TIME LEAVES SHADOWS	*65*
YOU COME WITH YOUR POWER	*66*
YOUR LOVE	*67*
FORGIVENESS BRINGS HEALING	*68*
PART THREE	69
AGELESS TIME	*72*
YEARS OF YESTERDAY	*73*
HIS GOLDEN LIGHT	*74*
GRANDSTANDS OF HEAVEN	*75*
DIVINE GIVER	*76*
ETERNITY LIES WAITING	*77*
ONE IN THREE; THE TRINITY	*80*
THE POWER OF YOUR NAME	*81*

FAR BEYOND OUR DREAMS	*82*
CITIZENS OF HEAVEN	*83*
GOD'S STABILITY	*84*
CRADLE ME IN YOUR ARMS LORD	*85*
PART FOUR	86
SACRED GROUND	*89*
THE DIVINE	*90*
SACRIFICE	*91*
EASTER DAWN	*94*
BEHOLD THE RISEN LORD	*95*
IN AWE AND WONDER	*98*
CHRISTMAS LOVE	*99*
UNDER THE SHINING STAR	*100*
IN THE BEYOND	*101*

PREFACE

Two things I just wanted to say about this book are, why I started writing and how I came by the title.

I grew up in the 1950's-1960's in Adelaide, South Australia, my life was pretty simple but wonderful. I was very lucky to have a secure family life, and my Mum and Dad brought the family up to treat others with respect, do the right thing, be courteous, and respect your elders. We had a strict upbringing and even as adults our parents never criticized us but encouraged us to do our best in life. They were "Aussie battlers" but we always managed to make it through the tough times!

They were people of integrity and cared about others and instilled that into our family.

Church was a big part of our lives growing up. We went to Sunday School at an early age and progressed up through the appropriate groups as we got older.

Youth groups, camps and church anniversaries were all important to the whole family. We competed in church sports teams, basketball and tennis with other parishes across Adelaide. Life-long friendships were in the making and cherished golden memories to look back on that would never fade.

Bible stories, hymns and choruses were all part of getting to know Jesus. This nurturing finally led me to the day Jesus came knocking on my heart's door. Being filled with the Holy Spirit is something I will never forget and the overwhelming power of His love that filled my whole being and propelled me to the front of the hall to give my heart to Him. No words can fully describe the joy I felt. That was in February 1968, I was 14 years of age. He has been my Shining Light ever since, and lives within me always.

So I thank my beautiful Mum and Dad for the way they raised me and for the foundation of knowing Jesus' love.

AGELESS TIME

It was in His love that I started to write, in the autumn of 1993. My journey has brought me to this book "Ageless Time", because thinking of the enormity and great magnitude of God in His realm, His time is ageless, which is almost beyond our understanding!

"For through him God created everything in heaven and on earth, the seen and the unseen things, including spiritual powers, lords, rulers, and authorities, God created the whole universe through him and for him." Colossians 1:16 Good News Bible.

God's Eternity is endless, it will never change and neither will He.

When I was a young Christian reading my Bible was really important to me in getting to know Jesus as my personal Saviour and became the foundation that I built my faith on.

It gave me strength and courage as I began life in the workforce at the age of 16. Coming from a sheltered upbringing it was my lifeline to self-confidence and adapting to social life at work.
The poems reflect the everyday feelings and emotions that we feel as we meet the challenges of life and how the great magnitude of God's love can help us rise above them.

I pray you will turn to Him not only in your hour of need but in celebration of happy times in your everyday life. He longs to be your Saviour and confidante so you can share everything with Him. The "One and Only" God Himself!

Many of these writings have been my first words of whispered prayer, so much that I have been moved to write them down at once and continue on in His wonderful and absolute love.

Together we write as He provides my inspiration.

All glory to Him, my precious Lord Jesus!

ACKNOWLEDGEMENTS

My heartfelt thanks to my beloved family, my Mum and Dad, Lilly and Ken, and my siblings Jeanette, June, Carol, Gloria and Lynne, for their never ending encouragement and support to me. To the rest of the family, you are all a precious link that joins us together.

To Michael and Andrew for your continual support to me in fulfilling my passion of writing poems for the Lord to help others through His Word.

A huge thank you to Junie for editing my poems and the coffees and lunches we enjoyed along the way.

A special big thank you to Joshua Woskett for his magnificent Moon cover photo and other Moon photos throughout the book. Such a joy to look at!

To Joy Furnell for her Crown of Thorns drawing, you have an amazing gift, thank you Joy.

A big thank you also to Lynne, Allan and Barry for great photos.

To my friends and Church Families, thank you for your love and support.

To my beautiful sons, Michael and Andrew, thank you for loving me, and I am so glad He gave you to me. I will love you forever. To your partners Andrea and Bianca and also my grandchildren, I love you all so much.

To you the reader, thank you for picking this book up and I pray you will find His peace and love on the pages ahead.

May He shower you all with His love and blessings.

PART ONE

"…everything God does will last forever. You can't
add anything to it or take anything away from it.
And one thing God does is to make us have reverence for him."

Ecclesiastes 3 : 14

AGELESS TIME

THE MOON…
STIRS HEART AND SOUL…

"So God made the two larger lights, the sun to rule over the day and the moon to rule over the night; …"

Genesis 1 : 16

MY DAILY PRAYER

Be with me, stay with me,
Close by my side,
Fill me with Your peace and love,
So my spirit shall surely fly
To the heights in Your love,
As only You can give,
Prepare me for this day ahead,
So in me You'll always live.

THE WONDERS OF THIS WORLD

Its formation unimaginable
That we see now,
A force of great magnitude
We can only wonder how.

So perfect and surreal
Mother Nature at her best,
The seasons that evolve
She is given Winter rest.

The Lord gave her gifts,
Earth's treasures to reveal,
Gems beneath the surface
And rolling carpets over the hills.

Rivers for her thirst,
Shade for noonday sun,
Plains for crops to grow
And harvest 'til day is done.

The wonders of this world Lord
Leave me in awe,
Your creation to behold
Touches me right to the core.

THE GLORY OF SUNRISE

The glory of sunrise,
Pure joy explodes,
Colour magnified
To thrill the senses so.

Moments of ecstasy
Is sunrise on the move,
Climbing high above
Brings His majesty to you.

Peace so overwhelming
Greets the soul,
Glory at sunrise
For you to behold.

Keep reality at a distance
For a few moments each day,
Watching the glory of sunrise
Will take your cares away.

HOUR GLASS

Our lives are like an hour glass
As the days seem to fly,
Time never stops counting
Governed by every sunrise.

This day will never come again
Sure enough that's true,
Our lives are precious to the Lord,
He wants the best for you.

He craves your sole attention
For His companionship alone,
You'll never know the depth
Of His love that you can own.

The years pass by so quickly
Like the sands in the hour glass,
Call Him into your life
Don't let Him go past.

All the hours in the centuries
We could never count that high,
But the hours in the hour glass
Will again never come by.

One thing is for certain,
We will never need
An hour glass in God's eternity,
In ageless time we will be!

KNOWING YOU IS LOVING YOU

Knowing You is loving You,
My heart tells me so,
The joy You give to me
Surely overflows.

Your love is so pure
Nothing can compare,
Knowing You is loving You,
Your message I have to share.

A revelation will take place
And turn your life around,
His Spirit will abide in you,
His gift so profound.

Knowing You is loving You,
The truth I have to tell,
How You came to save us,
You took the Cross for all the world.

PEACE IN MY HEART

There's peace in my heart
From my Father above,
My Saviour He lives
To shroud me in His love.

I ask Him to lay
His sweet love on me,
Bringing His peace
That keeps me feeling free.

He is my foundation,
The rock in my life,
Without Him I am nothing,
Challenges I could never survive.

His peace is enduring,
Forever my gift,
His love in my heart
Tells me He lives!

NO BOUNDARIES

Refresh my thoughts Dear One
To Your heights above,
Leaving earthly cares behind
To think of You, The Son.

My glorious risen Lord,
How I worship Thee,
You fill my heart with love
That knows no boundaries.

No boundaries of loving You
Below the stars above,
You shine brighter than the sun
In Your Heaven of love.

So precious Lord come to me
From the heights of Eternity,
Move my soul within
While I'm here in reality.

APPOINTED TIME

When life seems a puzzle
Nothing seems clear,
Go with your heart
He holds you so dear.

Knowing the Saviour
The precious Son above,
All in His appointed time
The answers will come.

Foggy days may drift in
When the sun can't shine,
The Holy Spirit will help you
To clear the way in time.

Worry doesn't help
But it seems that's what we do,
All will come to pass
In His appointed time for you.

AGELESS TIME

ETERNAL GOD…
ONLY YOU CAN…

"A thousand years to you are like one day; … "

Psalm 90 : 4

PERFECT

A rose on the vine
Thrills the senses so,
The Master's design,
Take a moment you will know.

No words can describe
The sweet perfume in the air,
A garden full of fragrance,
God lingers there!

The Lord's design is perfect
In shape and form,
Brings true delight
In the bud that He formed.

Like the Saviour's love
Perfect in every way,
A heart of pure gold
From you is what He craves.

LOVE HIM

Love Him with a burning desire
To serve Him all your days,
Nothing is impossible
When you love Him in all ways.

His rewards come from acts of kindness
That you bestowed that day,
Qualities He measures
To bring them your way.

His love will forge a will
Inside you so strong,
To change your heart forever
Where these gifts in you belong.

You are His son or daughter,
That's why He loves you so much,
With a love so deep and pure,
That brings His Holy Spirit's touch.

MY PEACEFUL HEART

I receive Your sweetness Lord
As I walk in Your light,
My peaceful heart anointed
With Your love that makes life bright.

Your shining light cleanses
And guides me so,
Your warmth wraps around me
To lead me on I know.

Thank You Lord for Your blessings
And the gifts You pour on me,
My peaceful heart rejoices
When I walk with Thee.

I only have to ask
For peace and calm in my life,
A feeling in my heart
The Holy Spirit provides.

UNTARNISHED LOVE

Nothing can tarnish the love
Of Jesus Christ my Lord,
Accepting Him into my heart
Together we are of one accord.

I refuse to let this love pale
On days that seem so dim,
No matter how I'm feeling
I must keep my eyes on Him.

Though dark shadows cross my path
His light still shines on me,
To reveal His guiding hand
That will lead me to Eternity.

In love we rejoice together,
In adoration I fall to my knees,
Our love will never tarnish
In all Eternity.

REFLECTION OF THE HEART

The reflection of the heart
Is so boldly seen,
In actions and words
Revealed by our deeds.

The reflection of the heart
Shines on the soul,
The home of His Spirit
Where He makes us whole.

When compassion and kindness
Dwell in our hearts,
That's the Fruits of the Spirit
To enrich our daily path.

The reflection of the heart
When deep in His love,
Brings those rewards
From the Lord above.

We are now blessed by His Spirit
As temples of God,
Vessels of hope
That reflect His love.

SPREADING HIS LOVE

The Master Himself
Came to earth,
To show us how to love
Because He loved us first.

He commands that we
Care for each other,
No cause for greed
Just peace and calm to discover.

He made us in His image,
He is love itself,
Through compassion and kindness
He made His values felt.

He wants us to be
Disciples for Him,
So spreading His love
Is where we begin.

HEAVEN'S GIFTS

You shower us with gifts,
Gifts to bless our lives,
But the greatest gift of all
Is Your gift of eternal life.

Heaven's gifts are a blessing
That we can pass on,
Show His love today
Because His Spirit makes you strong.

Heaven's gifts abide
The centuries of time,
They come from Your hand,
They flourish in Your light.

Heaven's gifts so special
Because they come from You,
To make our lives worth living,
Each one You can renew.

FACE TO FACE

Face to face with Jesus,
No better place to be,
Face to face with Jesus
Your eyes one day will see.

Face to face with Jesus
The light of Heaven alone,
Will shine for all eternity
When you claim Him as your own.

Face to face with Jesus
Your cares will slip away,
Nothing else will matter
With you He'll always stay.

Face to face with Jesus
The jewel of Heaven's Crown,
Shining bright forever
Our home in Heaven is found.

Face to face with Jesus,
Bow lowly at His feet,
Seated at God's right hand
Upon His Holy seat.

THANK YOU FATHER GOD

Thank You father God
For Your precious Son,
He reigns in His glory
So one day we can be one.

You gave Him authority
Over all the earth and space,
The wonders of the universe,
You called them into place.

His glory is in the Heavenlys
Known only to Heaven's Hosts,
He sits at the right hand of God,
Preparing our eternal home.

We thank You Father God
For our King of Kings,
Our Counsellor and our Saviour,
His glorious love He brings.

GOD'S TRUE LOVE

God's true love is waiting
To bless you through and through,
It comes with grace and mercy,
Your heart and soul renewed.

God's true love lasts forever,
His time has no end
Like a showering fountain,
His blessings He will send.

God's true love is ageless
From centuries ago,
In His power and His glory
That forever overflows.

God's true love adores you,
His invitation is for all,
His love will thrill your heart,
Answer when He calls.

THE SAVIOUR'S MESSAGE…
IS FOR EVERYONE…

"For what my Father wants is that all who see the Son and believe in him should have eternal life. …"

John 6 : 40

UNSPEAKABLE LOVE

Unspeakable love from Heaven
Is His Spirit who comes to abide,
He descends from Almighty God,
Pure peace in Him you will find.

Emotion beyond words
Will come to open your soul,
Where it will bloom like a flower
As His eternal love unfolds.

Unspeakable love is yours,
Ask Jesus into your heart
To receive His blessings for life,
So you can make a new start.

Unspeakable love is eternal
From Jesus Christ our Lord,
King of Kings forever,
You will want to love Him more.

Unspeakable love keeps on bursting
Like sweet buds on the vine,
Through the Holy Spirit's presence
When you know the Lord Divine.

ABUNDANT LOVE

Thank You dear one
For the abundance of Your love,
No words can explain
Your wonder above.

The abundance of Your love,
A never ending flow,
Stirring deep within,
Pure rapture I know.

No earthly riches
Though precious and rare,
Can compete with the joy
Felt when You are there.

Lord, Your abundant love
Brings peace, strength and calm,
Shrouding me forever
In Your loving arms.

So thank You precious One
For all You give,
And for sending Your Spirit
To abide within.

PAGES OF MY HEART

The pages of my heart Lord
Turn over every day,
My course in life woven
By the plans that I made.

Some are worn and creased,
Some are torn in two,
Some read over and over
Some when I listened to You.

My shame of all Lord
Is when I went my merry way,
Never giving You a thought,
That was when I lost my way.

Life is ever changing
As I grow with the years,
The pages of my heart
Have seen laughter and tears.

The longest chapter of them all
Is the lessons I have learnt
And the prompts from Your Spirit Lord,
To remind me how to serve.

So thank You precious Saviour
And Your Holy Spirit within,
You are with me on this journey
From the beginning to the end.

CLING TO HIS LOVE

Cling to God's love in all ways,
His truth will be known,
Your faith will grow and mature
In this you will be shown.

Cling to His love in all things,
His light will shine on you,
You will know eternal love
For He will guide you through.

Cling to His grace and mercy,
Strive to do what's right,
Through faith you will receive
His gift of eternal life.

His Spirit will abide in you,
His radiance shrouding your soul,
His perfect love you will know
For He has made you whole.

PART TWO

"…When the time came for me to show you favor, I heard you; when the day arrived for me to save you, I helped you.…"

2 Corinthians 6 : 2

AGELESS TIME

ALL GLORY TO OUR ETERNAL GOD… GIVER OF ETERNAL LIFE…

"I am telling you the truth: whoever hears my words and believes in him who sent me has eternal life. He will not be judged, but has already passed from death to life."

John 5 : 24

HEALING WILL UNFOLD

When you've been hurting
The strain takes its toll,
Healing will begin
Through time it will unfold.

Jesus is always there
To comfort and console,
Whisper your pleas for help
His healing will unfold.

He sees into your heart
And longs to anoint the scars,
He can help you heal yourself
If you turn to His open arms.

He will journey with you,
You are never alone,
Let Him heal your hurts
Because your heart He owns.

WHITE BUTTERFLIES

White butterflies bring peace
And calm along the way,
To lift a lonely spirit
To brighten their day.

White butterflies so delicate,
Fragile in every way,
Just like our lives
Feel bruised some days.

In Jesus Christ our Lord
We have strength for every day,
We are so delicate like butterflies,
But we can claim victory in His name!

So when you see a butterfly
Reflect on its delicacy,
Fragile but resilient
Just like you and me.

BE MY VOICE

Be my voice Lord
So love and compassion will show,
As a child of God
Because You I know.

May I have a light step
And a thankful heart,
Think twice before I speak
So Your words I can impart.

Be my voice Lord,
Take away my pain,
Help me to be silent,
When nothing I will gain.

Be my voice Lord
When I need to give a helping hand,
Give me Your words
So others can understand.

Be my voice Lord
Every day of my life,
May I be worthy
Of Your crown for life.

HIS PATH

The Lord sends His love
To every open heart,
Willing to accept
And travel His path.

His path is strewn
With compassion and care,
Kindness and love
You will find there.

Unload your worries
Fears and doubts,
You don't have to carry them,
These you can live without.

Stroll His path
Each day of your life,
His rapture you will find
When you walk in His light.

I NEED YOU LORD

My emotions are tossed about
Like a wild sea,
To get through today
I need Your stability.

Your shining light I need
To direct my path,
My needs You supply Lord
When I humbly ask.

I see You in my prayers Lord
That I offer to You,
I pray Your will be done,
To always see me through.

So though my needs may be many
I still offer them to You,
I need You Lord always,
To show me Your point of view.

KEEP A FAITHFUL HEART

Keep a faithful heart
For the King of Kings,
He requires your compassion
For everyday He brings.

Just a smile or a word
Can chase shadows away,
For someone who feels low
On a rainy day.

Keep a faithful heart
His Spirit will make you shine,
His light from Eternity
Will last the length of time.

Keep a faithful heart
You are always in His care,
He will reward you with a crown
Because His love today you shared.

AGELESS TIME

ALWAYS OUR SHEPHERD…
FOR ETERNITY…

"My sheep listen to my voice; I know them, and they follow me. I give them eternal life, and they shall never die. No one can snatch them away from me."

John 10 : 27, 28

VALUES OF THE HEART

We can cleanse our thoughts in life
When we talk to Christ our Lord,
He can remove the darkest stain
If Him we will adore.

The Lord looks at the heart
And values that lay within,
He measures by peace and kindness,
Not by wealth and gain to win.

We make our own choices
Whether wrong or right in His eyes,
Some may work out
But His will comes to light.

The values of the heart
Are trust and faith indeed,
His mercy and grace are yours
To help you to succeed.

He is the only way
For true values of the heart,
He is love itself,
On you He will leave His mark.

YOUR LIGHT

I am Yours forever Lord
Because I'm Your child,
One day when we meet
I will see Your heavenly smile.

Your light so bright
Will shine forever more,
Those who love You Lord
You will meet on Heaven's shore.

Your light will consume
Each one who loves You so,
Your power and Your glory
Will be revealed I know.

But for now my journey's here
As I pass through my life,
The promise when I believe,
Is I will receive eternal life!

I'M SO GLAD I'M YOURS LORD

I'm so glad I'm Yours Lord,
Your love that You've shown
My heart and soul shine
Because me, You own.

Your precious Holy Spirit
Brings words to my mind,
To share with Your beloved,
Your love I just can't hide.

I'm so glad I'm Yours Lord,
You calm the storms in me,
I need You by my side
To help with reality.

I'm so glad I'm Yours Lord,
You called me long ago,
the gift of Your Spirit
comforts me so!

CROSS THE BRIDGE TODAY

Enjoy every sunrise
Though a shadow may be falling today,
Your heart He will caress
To help you through this day.

Claim His strength to overcome
And cross the bridge today,
Though we are fragile
In faith we will find a way.

He is the lover of your soul
And He knows your steps in life,
Though the bridge is long and narrow
He is there to cast His light.

Weakness can turn to strength,
In Him you can surely rise
To cross that bridge with hope
As you approach the other side.

You'll look back and wonder why
And how you made it through,
Tomorrow there's another sunrise,
Jesus will be there for you.

I'M FOLLOWING YOU LORD

When life seems difficult,
Decisions to be made,
Call on the Master,
Don't be afraid.

Draw on your faith,
Trust and grace,
Believe you will be shown
In His time and place.

When I don't know what to do,
I turn to His Word,
I feel revived and loved
It helps me through.

Answers I find
To restore my faith,
I try to focus again
On His mercy and grace.

So when you feel lost
And think "nobody cares",
Turn to the Saviour
He's always there.

FIND A SAFE PLACE

Find a safe place
Inside your heart,
A place to go to
When anxiety starts.

Call for His peace and calm
When you feel afraid,
Believe He is there
To give you strength that day.

Find a safe place
To refresh your thoughts,
To dispel and soothe
Feelings of wrought.

Reach for His Word
Comfort you'll find,
His book on life
For a troubled mind.

Find a safe place
Be healed with His love,
Confess your hurts
To God above.

AGELESS TIME

THE SAVIOUR…
ALL GLORY FOREVER AND EVER…

"And eternal life means to know you, the only true God, and to know Jesus Christ, whom you sent."

John 17 : 3

LIFE'S PRESSURES

Life's pressures take their toll,
The weight too heavy to bear,
The mind and heart grow weary,
Still hope is always there.

Your faith and trust will tell you
A light still shines on you,
The Saviour knows your burden,
Ask Him to help you through.

His Word is always there,
His love a treasure to find,
His hand is upon you,
The answer will come in time.

Take life's pressures to the Saviour,
Commit to earnest prayer,
His Spirit will come with comfort,
Your heart will know He's there.

HUMANITY

Precious Holy Spirit
You bring us to our knees,
You bring Jesus' love
To all humanity.

Precious Holy Spirit
No words can explain
Your love in all its fullness,
That will never fade.

The cries of humanity
Never cease day or night,
Lord please help us look
To Your healing and light.

Through the Holy Spirit
Your love remains on earth,
For all mankind
You truly came to serve.

Every day we are renewed
By Your Spirit alone,
You crave for us
To make our heart Your home.

LIVING IN TRUST

I'm living in trust with God
Relying on His love,
Giving way for divine power
That I'm waiting on.

I'm waiting in trust with God,
Doors will open for me,
In His appointed time
His will for me I'll see.

Days may be barren
But the sun will surely rise,
I'm living in trust with God,
On Him I must rely.

I search my heart for prayers,
What more can I say?
I'm living in trust with God,
He knows my every day.

I'm living in trust with God
Because I love Him so,
I just have to patient,
His plan for me will show.

LIVE BY THE HEART

It's important to me
In the rush of life,
To make time for the Lord,
Each morning and night.

He brings His great love
It's there every day,
He's waiting patiently
For the prayers that I say.

I whisper a prayer
To commit the day,
"Lord help me to bear
What comes my way."

Help me to be
Your child of Light,
To live by the heart
And do what is right.

LESSONS OF LIFE

The lessons of life
Can leave their mark,
Some harsh, some kind,
In time will change the heart.

Actions and words leave an impression
That we're not always ready for,
But living in His love
Will prepare you even more.

Commit to rising above
The obstacles of life,
Claim His love and victory,
Walk in His light.

His lessons in life aren't easy
But we learn and move on,
Each step is growth,
The Saviour can make you strong.

The greatest teacher of all
Came quietly with His love,
We learn by the lessons of life
If we use our faith and trust.

LISTEN TO YOUR HEART

Listen to your heart
When doubts fill your head,
Ask the Saviour to show you,
Be sure you will be led.

He stands for truth and grace
And a faithful heart,
The Holy Spirit will speak
So listen to your heart.

Claim His help today
To rise above your fears,
He wants you to be happy,
He'll dry those falling tears.

Listen to your heart
Where His Holy Spirit lives,
Acknowledge His presence in your life,
His blessings He will give.

PRAISE OUR ETERNAL FATHER…

"To the eternal King, immortal and invisible, the only God – to him be honor and glory forever and ever! Amen."

1 Timothy 1 : 17

SAY "YES" TO JESUS

Say "yes" to Jesus
When you hear His prompts,
You are chosen to be His child,
In Him you will never want.

His Holy Spirit will provide
All that you need,
Your loving heart will respond
To sow His heavenly seeds.

God comes quietly
To change your heart,
Your values in life renewed
To reveal His commands.

So whisper these precious words
To invite the Saviour into your life,
"Come into my heart Lord Jesus
I am precious in Your sight."

MY CONSTANT COMPANION

My Saviour, my Lord,
My eternal Father always,
The steps that I take
May they be Yours today.

You are my constant companion
Through my ups and downs,
Where my life takes me,
Your shelter can be found.

Though some days I may be distant
With challenges of life,
But You are always my anchor
To keep me sublime.

My constant companion
I cannot live without,
In sunshine or in storm,
You; I can never doubt!

You are my constant companion,
I've learnt over the years,
I need You more than ever
Because to me, You are so dear.

NEVER GIVE UP

Reach for His Word for comfort,
He will lift your cares and fears,
Find His words of love
That will bring Him near.

Daily life can impact
Your thoughts through the day,
Stay strong in the Saviour,
Ask Him to show you the way.

But if you don't know Him,
He's longing for you to share,
He's waiting for your whispers,
To show you He cares.

Never give up on your trust and faith,
No matter how tough life gets,
He can do anything,
Go to Him for strength.

Never give up on hope,
Look to the Saviour above,
He cares for you constantly
Give Him your love.

PILLAR OF LIGHT

Sometimes You seem distant Lord
When I need You the most,
But my faith is still strong and true
In my eternal Heavenly Host.

I struggle to feel at peace
With doubts that fill my head,
I keep my eyes on You Lord
Knowing my needs will be met.

So when I feel You distant,
You haven't left my side,
It's my morality
That makes me want to hide.

Unite our Holy love Lord,
Restore my strength in You,
You are my pillar of light Lord,
Lead me on to peace in You.

RISE ABOVE YOUR FEARS

Don't listen to your inner voice
When doubts fill your mind,
Claim victory in Jesus,
Confidence you will find.

Rise above your fears
To His shining light,
Don't give in to failure,
You are precious in His sight.

You can succeed
To have a happy heart,
Strive to be positive
That's where you can start.

You will receive His strength
In His Holy Word,
Rise above your fears,
Your prayers are always heard.

LOVE HIM WITH ZEAL

The love of Jesus
Will make you feel
An overwhelming power
To love Him with zeal.

His love lies deep within
And will change your heart,
As you journey through life
His love will leave a mark.

He is the Prince of Peace
And "love" itself,
In Him we are complete
If we give ourselves.

A love that knows no end
Will come to command
Your life in its fullness
When you reach for His arms.

Surrender to Him
You will love Him with zeal,
Open your heart
His ways He will reveal.

When you meet with the Saviour,
Know wonders beyond your dreams,
You will love Him with zeal,
He's all you'll ever need!

WORTHY OF YOUR NAME

The testing times of living Lord
Bring anger, fear and doubt
With anxiety and sadness,
These we can live without.

To be worthy of Your name Lord
We have to curb these changing moods,
By praying for peace and calm
Is all we have to do.

Morality takes its toll,
Many lessons to be learnt,
The Saviour demands love and peace
That's why He came to serve.

Forgive us when we feel shame
And remorse fills our soul,
Take our sin away Lord,
Only You can make us whole.

RISE IN HIS GLORY

Rise in His glory,
Claim His peace and calm,
His grace and His mercy
I receive into my heart.

His light shines upon me
To heal my wounds and flaws,
I'm moved by His Spirit
Who loves me to the core.

Rise in His glory
Above the strains of life,
Connect with the Saviour,
The world's true, pure light.

Rise in His glory
To everlasting life,
In His power and awe,
My ever shining light.

TIME LEAVES SHADOWS

Time leaves shadows
Of memories that will fade,
Life unfolds like a flower,
Worn by the years of yesterday.

Years of shadows can speak volumes,
Life comes and goes
Into our hearts so deep,
The dreams and joys we know.

Shadows once so real,
Only now a memory in time,
The Saviour knew them all,
He will heal this heart of mine.

Time leaves shadows
That only the Master can wipe away,
Open your heart for His care,
So He can restore you today.

YOU COME WITH YOUR POWER

When I'm in a crisis Lord
You come with Your power,
With Your hand to anoint me
In my need that hour.

You come with Your power
So silent but real,
Your balm will heal
The wounds that I feel.

You come with Your power
Then the healing begins,
With my faith and trust
My heart soothed within.

You already know my future
On Your strength I can rely,
You come with Your power
To my heart you will supply.

YOUR LOVE

Your love is so deep Lord,
Words can't explain,
How You changed my life
And that You're here to stay.

Your love is so complete,
It brings eternal life,
You are precious Lord,
My eternal shining light.

Your love spans all time,
Born only from You,
From the creation,
You make things brand new.

Your love cleanses sin,
Forgives the deepest hurt,
It mends broken hearts,
The world, You came to serve.

Your love is everything,
Help me to see
You in Your Majesty
As You bring Your love to me.

FORGIVENESS BRINGS HEALING

When carrying a hurt
You think will never heal,
Only God can mend
The sorrow you feel.

The heart reacts
With pain and grief,
When a hurt you can't forgive
Makes your soul weep.

In our own human strength
We fail to see,
The hope of forgiveness
To set us free.

Only through the Holy Spirit
Can we receive
His power and love
For the forgiveness we need.

With faith so deep
In the Saviour's love,
Forgiveness brings healing
From God above.

In His love you can forgive,
The reward is yours,
Forgiveness brings healing,
His heavenly Hosts will applaud.

PART THREE

"…We live in union with the true God-in union with
his Son Jesus Christ. This is the true God,
and this is eternal life."

1 John 5 : 20

AGELESS TIME

REACH OUT …
TO HIS ETERNAL ARMS OF LIGHT…

"…Now God's home is with mankind! He will live with them, and they shall be his people. God himself will be with them, and he will be their God."
"He will wipe away all tears from their eyes. There will be no more death, no more grief or crying or pain. The old things have disappeared."

Revelation 21 : 3, 4

AGELESS TIME

His ageless time is perfect,
It unfolds at His behest,
There is a beginning
But there never is an end.

This age is pure,
One day we will understand,
Don't worry how to get there
For the Saviour will take your hand.

He will lead you by crystal waters
And down streets paved with gold,
His glory will shine everywhere
In His light for you to behold.

This age is eternal,
There's nothing you will lack,
All you need is Jesus
There's no need to look back.

No earthly words can describe
The wonders of His ageless time,
The Holy One is waiting
To show you Paradise!

YEARS OF YESTERDAY

Some lives are now slower
The fullness has passed away,
Time now to reflect
On the years of yesterday.

Church was so important
In the years of yesterday,
Sunday School for the children,
Bible stories along the way.

Memories to hold dear,
Many that will never fade,
Years that carved our heritage,
The years of yesterday.

Personal joys and sorrows
Meet everyone,
With faith and trust in God
He will help us rise above.

It's who we are that matters
All along the way,
Looking back through your life,
The years of yesterday.

The Lord knows our yesterdays,
He took the Cross to set us free,
No matter what's in our tomorrows,
He'll be with us constantly.

HIS GOLDEN LIGHT

His golden light will touch you
And take you to the heights,
Rapture so divine
Will fill you with delight.

His presence will surround you,
Your soul will glow within,
Meeting with the Saviour
A new life will begin.

His golden light so pure
Will touch you to the core,
Joy you've never known
Will make you love Him more.

His golden light will shine
Like a beacon far and wide,
Bringing untold wonder
That will bring Him to your side.

GRANDSTANDS OF HEAVEN

The grandstands of Heaven
Will stand for eternity,
They hold Your beloved, Lord
As they praise and worship Thee.

The grandstands of Heaven
Sparkle with the purest gems ever found,
Exquisitely displayed,
Angels singing so profound.

The grandstands of Heaven,
Always open to receive new guests,
Shining white robes adorn them
When they arrive for eternal rest.

The grandstands of Heaven,
A reflection of the Saviour's light,
A brilliance never seen
Because His glory is so bright.

The grandstands of Heaven
Roar for the King of Kings,
His power and glory revealed,
Majesty and awe He brings.

The grandstands of Heaven
Will surely be something to see
When we come into His presence
To take our place in eternity.

DIVINE GIVER

Divine Giver; Lord of all
You made all we see,
Precious Lord Jesus
You beckon us to follow Thee.

Divine Giver; Prince of Peace
You bring humility,
The simple things of life
Are all we truly need.

Divine Giver; Wonderful Counsellor
You hear our every call,
King of Mercy and Grace,
Help us to stand tall.

Divine Giver; King of Kings
Upon Your Throne of Light,
You are eternal,
We are precious in Your sight.

Divine Giver; King of Glory
Eternal Father You truly are,
Our home You've prepared in the Heavens
When we journey beyond the Stars.

ETERNITY LIES WAITING

Lord, as members of Your family
Your glory awaits,
Within Your Holy household
Lies Eternity to take.

A home on Heaven's shore
That no earthly eyes can see,
A home of pure love
Waits for His family.

Gifts unimaginable are there
At Your sacred Throne,
Rewards to open
When the Saviour calls us home.

His heavenly hosts are waiting
To welcome us that day,
Those gifts we will receive
For His commands that we obeyed.

Yes, Eternity lies waiting
With raptures by the score,
God's forever home for us
When we step on Heaven's shore.

THE MAGNIFICENCE...
OF HIS GLORY...

"This God is our God forever and ever;
he will lead us for all time to come."

Psalm 48 : 14

ONE IN THREE; THE TRINITY

One in Three; The Trinity,
Divine Kingship and authority,
Serve us with their love
For all humanity.

Touching the open soul,
Waiting for it to respond
To Your heavenly touch,
From Your Spirit it comes.

Your anointing takes place
To change and cleanse the heart,
Your light shines within
With a love that will never depart.

Steeped in love divine
Your faith and trust will grow,
One in Three; The Trinity
Their love to you they'll show.

THE POWER OF YOUR NAME

The power of Your name Lord,
Makes me bow in reverence,
I bring my prayers to You
In Your ageless Heaven.

Precious Holy Lord,
My earthly cares minute,
Your promised gifts are waiting
In ageless time from You.

The power of Your name
Brings me to my knees,
My Holy, Eternal Father
You, one day I'll see.

So thank You precious Lord
You are the true "I Am",
Holy You'll always be,
I long to hold Your hand.

The eyes of the world
Will look to You one day,
On the day You return
In the power of Your name!

FAR BEYOND OUR DREAMS

I know a love
That can take me beyond
The realms of life
To the heavens above.

The Lord in His fullness
Shares His love,
Far beyond our dreams
Is our home above.

A place where cares
No longer exist,
All we will know
Is Heaven's perfect bliss.

The Lord Jesus Himself
Will welcome you there,
Far beyond your dreams
His love He will share.

A promise to all
Who receive Him as King,
When we meet our loved ones
Far beyond our dreams.

When we go beyond our dreams
We will meet the Lord of Heaven
Paradise will open
His rewards will be given.

CITIZENS OF HEAVEN

A citizen of Heaven
Shares the Lord's eternal light,
His love supremely reigns
In Heaven's ageless time.

Glorious heavenly voices
Fill the air with song,
With praises to the Lord
As they rejoice in garrison.

A citizen of Heaven
Only knows divine love,
Living in His presence
On Heaven's shore above.

Tears are gone forever,
Pain will not exist,
Living with the Lord
All believers are His.

Citizens of Heaven
Receive a Crown of Life,
Your rewards are waiting
When you are called into His Light!

GOD'S STABILITY

I need You every day Lord,
You; I can't live without,
I need Your stability
To shun those fears and doubts.

I have to remain positive
Even in the lows of my life,
But I have to look to You
And Your shining light.

I need You every day Lord,
My anchor and my rock,
You I can lean upon,
Our love will never stop.

Strengthen me in Your ways
Because I am Your child,
Together we are one,
Show me Your heavenly smile!

CRADLE ME IN YOUR ARMS LORD

Cradle me in Your arms Lord
To protect me all eternity,
Where Your pure love lives
I'll be face to face with Thee.

Cradle me in Your arms Lord
My heavenly Father You are,
My place of rest and slumber
Is the safety of Your arms.

Cradle me in Your arms Lord,
Never let me go,
My Saviour and my Father,
How I love You so!

Cradle me in Your arms Lord
As a father would his child,
I will know Your peace and calm,
I will see Your heavenly smile.

PART FOUR

"For God loved the world so much that he gave his only Son, so that everyone who believes in him may not die but have eternal life."

John 3 : 16

HOLY COMMUNION…
TO REMEMBER HIM FOREVER…

"Then he took a piece of bread, gave thanks to God,
broke it, and gave it to them, saying, "This is my body,
which is given for you. Do this in memory of me."
In the same way, he gave them the cup after the supper, saying,
"This cup is God's new covenant sealed with my blood, which
is poured out for you."

Luke 22 : 19, 20

SACRED GROUND

No problem is too complex,
No solution that can't be found,
No way is hidden
When you stand on sacred ground.

Jesus' Cross goes before you,
The gateway to His Throne,
A sacrifice He made
So you could be His own.

His Cross goes before you,
Every debt for you He paid,
Every stain upon you
His blood washed away.

His Cross is everything,
A symbol of new life
When the Lord redeemed us
When He was crucified.

God raised Him from the Tomb,
He's no longer in the grave,
The Cross is sacred ground
Where His life for you He gave!

THE DIVINE

His ministry began
Preaching His Word everywhere,
A three- year mission,
The Son of God; He declared.

He called His Apostles
To a Discipleship of love,
The precious few to know Him
And learn what was to come.

He calmed the storm,
Turned water into wine,
He healed the sick,
Performed miracles, the Divine.

The Divine; Lord Jesus,
Heaven's shining light,
Came to earth for one reason,
To sow seeds for eternal life.

He loved us so much,
He took our sin to Calvary,
The weight of the world,
He carried to set us free.

The Divine; Lord Jesus
King of Kings and Lord of Lords,
His reign will never end,
But it's you He adores!

SACRIFICE

The weight of this world
Is sometimes more than we can bear,
But You took the Cross Lord
To show how much You cared.

You loved us all completely
That You died to give us life,
After three days in the Tomb
You rose from death to life.

Your Hands still bear the marks
Of the sacrifice You made,
Can we ever understand
The eternal life You gave.

We can never thank You
Enough for Your sacrifice,
You took the Cross
To give us Eternal Life!

AGELESS TIME

FOREVER AND EVER …
HE LIVES…

"I am the living one! I was dead,
but now I am alive forever and ever. …"

Revelation 1 : 18

EASTER DAWN

Forever joy today,
The Saviour freed from the Tomb,
Forever joy today,
He lives for me and you.

The Crown of Thorns replaced,
No more heartache to mourn,
He now wears a Crown of Gold
With the coming of Easter Dawn.

The darkness of the grave
Overthrown with Heaven's light,
The grave now wide open,
Angels sing with pure delight.

His palms still bear the marks
Of the Sacrifice He bore,
To give us eternal life,
Hallelujah; It's Easter Dawn.

Easter Dawn; God's miracle
He raised His Son from the grave,
Easter Dawn; What joy,
He lives, He lives, today!

BEHOLD THE RISEN LORD

In the coolness of the morning
On the Third Day,
The Risen Christ was in the garden,
The stone now rolled away.

The bondage of death was broken,
God's power now revealed,
Behold the risen Lord,
Eternal Life was sealed.

Behold the risen Lord,
The grave clothes thrown away,
His wounds now healed,
But the marks on His hands remain.

His Sacrifice for the world,
For that one day at Calvary
Will never be repeated,
He took the Cross for you and me.

Behold the risen Christ,
All glory to His Name,
He overcame the world,
Now forever an empty grave!

AGELESS TIME

FOREVER CHRISTMAS JOY…
AWE AND WONDER…

"…The Holy Spirit will come on you, and God's power will rest upon you. For this reason the holy child will be called the Son of God."

Luke 1 : 35

IN AWE AND WONDER

The awe and wonder of Christmas
Is new every year,
We celebrate the birth of Jesus
Because to Him we are so dear.

The Christmas story from long ago
Still refreshes and restores
The joy in me like no other,
The birth of God's baby boy.

The angel's proclaimed His arrival
To the shepherds in the fields,
The Star shone bright over the Stable,
The heavens sparkling jewel.

In awe and in wonder
They followed the Star
Until it stopped above the Stable,
And the Wisemen came from afar.

The awe and wonder of Christmas
Will live forever in our hearts,
The miraculous birth of the Saviour
And the wonder of the eastern Star!

CHRISTMAS LOVE

Christmas love was heralded
By the angels above,
The heavenly hosts proclaimed
His glory and His love.

They came to the shepherds
To pronounce the Holy news,
A precious Babe lay in swaddling clothes
In the lowly mews.

A shining star so bright
In the night sky,
Stopped over the stable
That first Christmas night.

The Messiah brought Christmas love
To the world that night,
From the cradle He would grow
To be our Shining Light!

UNDER THE SHINING STAR

Under the shining star
The Messiah was born,
In a lowly stable
He saw His first Christmas dawn.

Under the shining star
Three Kings came from the East,
Bearing precious gifts
For the new born King.

Under the shining star
Glory shone down,
Holy angels sang with joy
Because His birth was so profound.

The Holy Messiah
Brought a Crown of Life
To the stable in Bethlehem
On that first Holy night.

IN THE BEYOND

I believe in the revelation
Of His Holy Word,
In the beyond only love
And angels singing will be heard.

In our forever home
We will live with God,
There will be no hardships
Only joy in the beyond.

I can only think of peace
And love everywhere,
No tears or pain
Or heartache to bear.

In the beyond, I think of
Crystal waters and flowing streams,
Glorious flowers and fields,
Colours, never seen.

In the beyond, magnificence,
Wonder and awe,
Gifts we can't imagine
Will be His rewards.

What glory awaits us,
His Majesty on His Throne
When we meet Jesus face to face
In our forever home!

ALSO BY CLAIRE GROSE

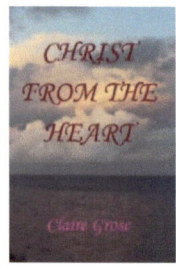 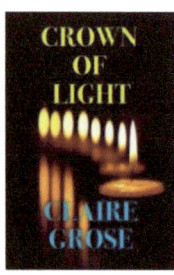 

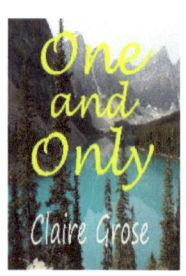 

ABOUT THE AUTHOR

Claire worked as a Government Public Servant in the Lands Department, Adelaide, South Australia until she married and became a mother of two boys.

She later returned to the work force during which time she gained a "Living Hope" Phone Counselling certificate which influenced her need to help others.

Through this and personal experience she found herself inspired by God's love to put pen to paper.

PHOTO CREDITS

COVER PHOTO: Moon Photo taken by Joshua Woskett

Page 2: Pink Supermoon; S.A. – Joshua Woskett
Page 12: Bottle Brush; S.A. – Claire Grose
Page 24: Waxing Moon; S.A. – Joshua Woskett
Page 31: Boab Trees; S.A. – Claire Grose
Page 39: Fremont Park; S.A. – Claire Grose
Page 47: Hastings Point; N.S.W. – Claire Grose
Page 55: Yucca Flowers; S.A. – Lynne
Page 70: Mallala Grandstand; S.A. – Claire Grose
Page 78: Moon Photo; – Joshua Woskett
Page 87: Croton Plant; N.S.W. – Allan and Barry
Page 92: Semaphore Beach; S.A. – Claire Grose
Page 96: Hibiscus Flowers; S.A. – Claire Grose

AGELESS TIME

www.ingramcontent.com/pod-product-compliance
Lightning Source LLC
Chambersburg PA
CBHW041500010526
44107CB00044B/1511